Chapter
Won

Every Ending Leads to a New Beginning

From the wounds to the awakening,
this journey teaches you how to gather your strength,
reclaim your story, and step into victory again and again.

By Brandy Martin

Chapter Won

A Letter to My Family,

Because Chapter Won Begins with You

To my family...
my first circle, my first home, my first teachers of love,

As I step fully into my *Chapter Won*, I cannot move forward without honouring those who held me long before I ever knew how to hold myself. This chapter, this becoming, is not just mine. You were the hands that guided me, the prayers that covered me, the love that carried me through the pieces of my life I didn't yet know how to name.

Before the healing, before the wings, before the woman I am today, there was a version of me who was hurting, breaking, surviving. And in that season, I know I bled on people who never cut me. I want to speak to that honestly, humbly, and from the healed place I stand in today.

To My Parents

Thank you for staying, even when it was hard.
Thank you for loving me through my mess, my mistakes, my confusion, my tears.
Thank you for covering me when the world pointed fingers, whispered gossip, and judged the child you raised.

I am so sorry for the shame and embarrassment my unhealed self, brought into your lives, through ignorance, through pain, through trying to navigate storms I didn't yet understand. You never stopped praying for me. You never stopped fighting for me.
You never stopped loving me.

You were my first intercessors, my first protectors, my first encounter with unconditional love. Your faith carried me, your love lifted me, you were the wind beneath my wings.

To My Brothers

Thank you for being my protectors,
in the flesh *and* in the spirit.

Thank you for listening when my voice shook,
for standing ten toes down when I felt weak,
for being ready to fight battles I had no strength to face.

Your love is fierce, loyal, and loud.
You have always made sure your **sister/ st-is-ter** knew she wasn't alone.

To My Husband

My love, my partner, my covering,
Thank you for choosing me.
Thank you for walking beside me through the storms and the sunshine.

Your wisdom steadied me.
Your guidance challenged me.
Your strength softened me.

You taught me how to operate from my feminine place,
how to be soft without being afraid,
how to trust without trembling,
how to love without shrinking.

Thank you for loving me in a way I once believed was impossible.

To My Children

My heartbeats...
My why...
My redemption story wrapped in skin...

There are no words big enough to hold the sorrow I've felt for the times I couldn't give you what you needed. Not out of lack of love, but lack of healing.
I was a mother trying to pour from an empty place, doing the best I could with what I had, but I know it wasn't always enough.

Thank you for forgiving me.
Thank you for growing with me.
Thank you for accepting my apologies, even when I didn't feel worthy of your grace.
You loved me through my breaking... and into my becoming.

I love you with every breath, every dream, every new beginning.
You are my legacy, my laughter, my lifeline.

To My Baby Girl, My Miracle

You are Heaven in human form.
Thank you for being you, pure, bold, brilliant, unstoppable.

You have taught me more than you will ever understand.
Your smile, your questions, your curiosity, they remind me daily why breaking generational curses matters.

I am healing because of you.
I am becoming because of you.

I am softening because you deserve a mother who knows her worth.
You are unstoppable, baby, and I am cheering for you with my whole soul.

To my wonderful bonus children,

Thank you for accepting me and loving me just as I am. Each of you is a precious jewel, and my life is brighter because of you. We've grown together in so many ways, and I am so grateful for every shared laugh, hug, and moment. Thank you for allowing me the honour of being not just a step, but a bonus mom in your lives. You have filled my heart in ways I could never have imagined, and I cherish each of you more than words can say.

To My Daughters, in, Loves

Thank you for putting up with us,
the jokes, the chaos, the "family crazy," and the love that comes with all of it.
You are beautifully woven into our story, and I honour the grace you bring into our lives.

To My Grand Boo's and Grand Bae Bae's

This book, this healing, this transformation,
is for you too.
Abi, loves you beyond words.
You all are my joy, my sunshine, my tender places in human form.

To My Student, ZyQuala

Thank you for inspiring me to write this.
You are a jewel, rare, brilliant, unforgettable.

Your honesty and encouragement sparked a fire in me I didn't even know still burned.

The sky is not the limit for you, it's just the starting point.

To My Family and Friends

I love you.
Thank you for staying.
Thank you for seeing me before I could see myself.

And To Anyone I've Ever Hurt

I apologize from a healed, honest place.
Not for telling my truth,
but for the wounds my unhealed season may have caused.

I have nothing left to hide.
I am free.
I forgive.
I am forgiven.

Because Chapter Won Begins with Gratitude

This book is not just my story, it's the story of everyone who prayed for me, held me, corrected me, fought for me, and loved me when I didn't love myself. You were there in my chrysalis. You saw the breaking, the becoming, and now the rising. I honor you, because I could not have reached Chapter Won without you turning the pages with me.

I see you.
I see your quiet battles, your storms, your strength, the moments you

thought you couldn't go on but still rose anyway. Every step, even the painful ones, has led you here.

Chapter Won is your mirror. A reminder that brokenness isn't final, darkness isn't permanent, and every "what, if" you've carried can now be laid to rest. Forgive yourself. Release the weight. You are worthy, whole, and free.

As you read, may you feel seen and empowered to begin again. Your wings are waiting.

With all my heart,
Brandy Martin

Table of Contents

The Journey Begins

*L*ife has a way of shaping us in ways we cannot always predict. Some moments bring joy, others bring heartbreak. Some experiences leave scars, some leave lessons, and every single one holds the quiet power to transform us.

This is my story. Not a story of perfection, not a collection of pretty moments tied together with neat bows. It is a story of survival, of breaking and rebuilding, of running away and finally returning to myself. It is about the storms I walked through, the weight I carried, and the faith that whispered to me when the world around me went silent. It is about stepping into the chrysalis, that sacred, shadowed place where everything old must fall apart before anything new can rise.

In that stillness, I confronted my pain, owned my choices, forgave myself, and began the slow, trembling emergence into the woman I was always meant to become.

But this story is more than memory, it is an invitation.

Just as a caterpillar's purpose is to feed, stretch, and survive, there were seasons of my life where I existed only to meet everyone else's needs. I poured out, gave away, shrank myself, and became a source of nourishment for people who did not always pour back into me. I served, I carried, I endured. But even caterpillars are not meant to stay in that stage forever.

The chrysalis comes next, the transformation, the healing, the great undoing and remaking. And healing is not a gentle process. It requires honesty. It demands stillness. It insists on truth. It calls you to look at everything you avoided, everything you hid, everything you tried to outrun. That is where I found myself: wrapped in darkness, suspended between who I had been and who I was becoming.

And when I finally emerged, broken open but whole, softer yet stronger, I understood that butterflies have a new purpose. They pollinate. They carry life. They spread beauty. They take what they have learned and share it, quietly blessing every place they touch. That is what this book is for me. That is what this journal is for you.

As you read my story, you will also be invited to write your own.

Throughout these pages, you will find moments to pause, reflect, breathe, and tell yourself the truth you may have avoided for years. These journal prompts are more than questions, they are mirrors. They will help you explore your own metamorphosis, honour the caterpillar you once were, embrace the chrysalis you may still be inside, and prepare for the wings waiting for you.

I want to be honest, yet I am also careful. People often want the "juicy" details, the betrayals, the secrets, the mistakes. But some things are sacred. Some memories are held close, protected, and left to the imagination. My journey is not about exposing wounds or reliving every painful moment. It is about growth. It is about healing. It is about the emergence that comes when you finally face yourself and choose yourself.

As you turn these pages, my hope is simple:

That you will see your past does not define you.
Your heartbreaks do not disqualify you.
Your mistakes do not cancel your purpose.
Your dark seasons are not your ending, they are your chrysalis.

Like me, you can rise.
Like me, you can heal.
Like me, you can discover your wings... and learn to fly.

Welcome to *Chapter Won, When the Last Chapter Ends, Your True Story Begins*
Welcome to the story of a woman who learned to choose herself.
And welcome to the journal that will help *you* choose you too.

Your journey begins now.
Your wings are already waiting.

Chapter One:
Because My Last Chapter Wasn't My Final Chapter

*Y*ou thought the last chapter was the end, but spoiler alert: it wasn't. It was the chrysalis, the quiet, messy, awkward, sometimes terrifying space before the wings could grow. This is my **Chapter Won**.

For years, I lived in a world where survival meant smiling through pain, praying through heartbreak, and convincing myself that if I loved hard enough, I could fix a man who was slowly breaking me. Before I was thirteen, I carried wounds too heavy for a child, molestation, shame, secrets, and judgment from the very people who were supposed to protect me. By my teens, I was facing a pregnancy and entering a marriage I had been warned against. And yes, I did it my way (cue Frank Sinatra), and yes, I paid in ways my heart still remembers. Spoiler alert: it was *not* the glamorous kind of "my way" you imagine. No tuxedos, no jazz band, just a lot of crying in the bathroom.

As a daughter, I grew up with parents who did the best they could to love and support me. They gave what they knew, offered what they had, and poured into me from their own wells. But even with all of that, I still carried an emptiness I didn't know how to name. There were places inside me that their love couldn't reach, spaces shaped by silence, shame, and unspoken hurt. And in trying to fill those spaces, I went searching for love in the wrong places, clinging to anyone who made me feel seen, even if it cost me pieces of myself.

What followed were years of abuse, betrayal, emotional abandonment, and a loneliness so deep it almost swallowed me whole. He cheated. He left. He returned... and repeated the cycle. Yet I stayed, not because love was real, but because shame was louder. I stayed because I believed the lie that broken was all I could ever be.

Until the day I finally told myself the truth: the only person I needed to fix was me.

With $70, trembling courage, and a thread of faith holding me together, I walked away. Leaving wasn't glamorous. It wasn't cinematic. It wasn't even Instagram, worthy (and yes, I briefly considered posting a dramatic caption anyway). It was survival. Necessary. The first breath after nearly drowning.

But freedom felt like stepping into darkness. Nights were suffocating, silence deafening. I hadn't lost money, I had lost identity, safety, and the version of myself I had clung to for years. This was my **Chapter 11, not financial bankruptcy, but spiritual and emotional restructuring.** A teardown. A rebuilding. A clearing out of everything that had kept me small.

Healing, I discovered, is like metamorphosis. A caterpillar exists to consume, to serve, to be nourishment for others. For years, that was me, feeding egos, sustaining dysfunction, carrying emotional weight, while slowly disappearing. Every caterpillar reaches its limit. Every caterpillar eventually stops. Every caterpillar enters the chrysalis.

The chrysalis looks like isolation. Feels like falling apart. But it is sacred. It is the place where the old dissolves so the new can form. And in that space, I learned the struggle is not punishment, it's preparation. Every heartbreak, every tear, soaked pillow, every night I thought I wouldn't survive... was strengthening my wings. I wasn't breaking down; I was forming.

Healing isn't straight. I stumbled. I reached for the wrong things. I numbed myself with busyness, people, noise. I failed my children at times. I poured from an empty soul. And yet, mercy always found me. Even when I didn't want to live, grace held me. Slowly, I rebuilt a relationship with myself, grounded in truth, not survival. I went back to school. Earned my bachelor's, my master's, and now I pursue my doctorate, not for anyone else, but for the little girl inside who never felt seen, smart, worthy, or loved. That daughter within me is finally being held by the woman I've become.

Education became part of my metamorphosis. Each degree strengthened my wings. And as I grew, love found me again. Different this time. Gentle. Steady. A man who offered safety where I had only known fear. We are not perfect; our love has storms. But together, we explore truth, softness, accountability, humility, and healing. I am learning to love openly, to trust without suspicion, to embrace my femininity and divine softness. Softness is not weakness. Softness is power.

My degrees are not trophies. My marriage is not a rescue. My healing is not linear. But everything I've walked through proves that a broken girl can rise when she chooses herself. This story is not about the pain, it's about the woman who survived it, the daughter reclaimed, the mother reclaiming her bond with her children, the wife learning to love without fear. The woman emerging from the chrysalis, wings stiff, heart trembling, ready to fly.

My last chapter was not my final chapter. It was the chrysalis. The breaking open. The restructuring of my soul.

And now, with softened strength, humour intact, and newly formed wings, I am ready to tell the truth:

I am free.
I am becoming.
This, this right here, is my **Chapter Won**.

 # Chapter One, Affirmation

Affirmations for My Becoming

Read these slowly. Let them settle into you.

- I honour the chapters that tried to break me, because they strengthened my wings.

- I am worthy of softness, safety, and love that nourishes me.

- I release what no longer aligns with who I am becoming.

- I trust the timing of my healing, even the slow, quiet parts.

- I am allowed to start again, and again, and again.

- My story is not over. I am still rising.

- I am reclaiming the pieces of me I once abandoned.

- I am becoming whole, even in small steps.

Chapter One, Guided Journal Prompt

"Dear Self... I See You"

Write a letter to yourself as if you were speaking to someone you deeply love.

Acknowledge:

- ✔ What you've survived

  _____

  _____

  _____

- ✔ How far you've come

  _____

  _____

  _____

- ✔ What you're ready to release

  _____

  _____

  _____

- ✔ What you hope to step into

  _____

  _____

  _____

Let it be honest. Let it be gentle. Let it be yours.

 Chapter One, Closing Encouragement

A Gentle Note for the Road Ahead

Before you turn to the next chapter, pause and honour this moment.
You've looked back with truth.
You've opened your heart with honesty.
You've acknowledged the weight you've carried, and the strength it took to carry it.

This is your chrysalis moment.
Not the end.
Not the breaking.
But the becoming.

Your wings are forming, even when you can't feel them.
Your future is stretching, even when the past still whispers.
And the beautiful thing is...
you don't have to rush.
You only have to keep showing up, softly, bravely, and as yourself.

Turn the page when you're ready.
A new chapter is waiting,
and this time,
you win.

Chapter Two:
The Egg: Foundations, Warnings & the Lessons I Couldn't Yet See

*B*efore a butterfly ever spreads its wings, its mother places the egg carefully on a leaf, a deliberate act of protection, intention, and hope. She places it where she believes life can begin safely, even though the caterpillar inside has no idea how fragile it truly is.

Parents are much the same. They place us on the "leaves" they believe will give us the best chance at life: guidance, structure, values, discipline, warnings, and love. They do the best they can with what they have. And like that tiny egg, we rarely understand the purpose behind their protection. We only feel the boundaries, not the love that built them.

My parents planted me in soil they believed would keep me safe. No, they weren't perfect. But they gave me discipline. They gave me direction. They gave me dreams bigger than my own. They gave me warnings. They gave me love. And for that, I am forever grateful, even when I didn't understand it at the time.

But no parent can predict the storms a child will face. No parent can walk every path for them. And no parent can stop a child determined to grow in her own way.

As I entered adolescence, my caterpillar years, I stretched far beyond every boundary my parents had set. Like every hard, headed caterpillar who believes it knows its own path, I thought I was ready for the world. I thought I had all the answers. I thought my parents didn't understand me.

I chased relationships they disapproved of. I craved attention I mistook for affection. I confused desire with destiny.

It was messy, complicated and painful, like living the lyrics of Kelly Price's As We Lay, doing wrong while still hoping it would become love. I found myself in an entanglement the world would later recognize through Will and Jada, with August caught in the middle, where power, affection, and silence blurred into something that looked like intimacy. I fell for illusions I wasn't emotionally equipped to navigate, unraveling in situations I was far too young to be in, mistaking survival for love and entanglement for choice.

My dad even offered to buy me a Lexus, not as a bribe, but as a desperate attempt to redirect my steps. He was trying to pull me away from a fire I insisted on playing in. But when your heart is set on the wrong thing, even wisdom feels like control. Even love feels like restriction.

If I could've seen through my parents' eyes, I would've moved differently. But I was young. Blind to danger. Hungry for validation. Certain I knew better.

Then came one of the darkest moments of my life. I was walking to the pharmacy, emotionally depleted, mentally worn down by abuse, and convinced the world would be better without me. I didn't want to die; I just didn't know how to live anymore. I felt ugly. Unworthy. Hopeless. Like everything inside, me was collapsing.

But right there on that sidewalk, my son, still so small, began to sing:

"Yes, Jesus loves me..."

His tiny voice cracked the darkness wrapped around me. Right there, I broke. Tears streamed down my face. Something inside whispered, *"Turn around."* And I did. My son saved my life that day.

Still, I had already tasted the poisoned apple, not from any fairytale, but the Snow, White kind of poison that comes from believing you're less than what you truly are. I thought poorly of myself long before anyone else had the chance to. I didn't recognize the light in me, even when others quietly did. It wasn't until I "bit the apple", until I ingested every lie about not being pretty enough, smart enough, wanted enough, that the poison settled in. And from that moment on, I slept on myself. I dimmed my own shine. I walked through life half, awake, surviving but not living, forgetting that I was meant for more. That poison pushed me into the chrysalis season: the season of hiding, shrinking, pretending... the season where I learned to smile while slowly disappearing inside myself.

I thought the makeup and wigs covered the bruises. I thought my smiles hid the suffering. I thought silence was strength.

But one day, a woman pulled my wig back, literally, exposing the bruises I worked tirelessly to hide. It felt humiliating. Violative. Intrusive. But now, looking back, it was the first moment the layers began to fall away. She didn't expose me. She revealed me, to myself.

Then came the wake, up call that shook my soul. My neighbour, a woman living a story far too close to my own, lost her life to the same violence I was enduring. She didn't make it out. Her children lost their mother. She was gone because of him, yet he turned away from the wreckage and walked straight into another woman's life...

Standing there, I knew that could've been me. That would have been me... if I didn't move.

Something inside me snapped, not in fear, but in clarity. Determination. Resolve. I decided my story would not end like hers. I would live. I would fight. I would crawl, inch by inch, out of the poison I had mistaken for love.

These were my caterpillar years: messy, painful, confusing, full of missteps and lessons learned the hardest way imaginable. These were the years where I grew in directions that hurt me, where I mistook chaos for passion and toxicity for intimacy, where my parents' wisdom felt restrictive instead of protective.

But caterpillars don't stay caterpillars forever. Even the stubborn ones. Even the broken ones. Even the ones who wander onto dangerous branches.

Sometimes it is the worst pain that becomes the soil of transformation.

Sometimes it is the storm that prepares you for wings you don't yet know you're growing.

 ## Chapter Two, Reflection

The Egg: Foundations, Warnings & the Lessons I Couldn't Yet See

Before you move forward, pause and let your heart settle.

This chapter reached into childhood, adolescence, pain, protection, and the early roots of your becoming.

These reflections will help you honour what shaped you, and what you've outgrown.

Reflection Questions

1. What did your parents, guardians, or early caregivers give you that you didn't understand then, but appreciate now?

   Think about boundaries, guidance, warnings, or love that made sense only in hindsight.

   _____

   _____

   _____

   _____

2. What early wounds or moments planted beliefs in you that you carried into adulthood?

   What "poisoned apples" shaped how you saw yourself?

   _____

   _____

   _____

3. What moment cracked the darkness for you, your "Yes, Jesus loves me" moment, when something or someone reminded you to turn back toward life?

_____

_____

_____

_____

Honor that turning point.

 Chapter Two, Affirmation

Affirmations for My Caterpillar Years

Read these slowly, letting them soften the parts of you that still remember the pain.

- ☑ I honour the child, teen, and young adult I once was, doing the best they could with what they knew.

- ☑ The boundaries I once resisted now reveal the love that shaped me.

- ☑ I release the lies I believed about my worth; they were never mine to carry.

- ☑ What tried to poison me became the soil that strengthened me.

- ☑ My past is a teacher, not a life sentence.

- ☑ I deserve safety, tenderness, and love that does not harm me.

- ☑ I see the light in myself now, even when I missed it then.

- ☑ I forgive myself for the years I lived half, awake. I am choosing myself now.

Chapter Two, Guided Journal Prompt

"To the Younger Me..."

Write a letter to your younger self, the caterpillar version of you.
Speak to them with tenderness. Tell them:

- ✓ What you understand now that they couldn't see

- ✓ The love and protection they didn't recognize

- ✓ The dangers they walked into without knowing

- ✓ The beauty, strength, and worth they always had

- ✓ The future they survived long enough to create

Let this be a letter of compassion, not correction.

✋ Chapter Two, Closing Encouragement

A Soft Word for Your Becoming

Your early years shaped you, but they did not define you.
You were placed carefully, even when the world felt dangerous.
You were loved, even when the protection felt like restriction.
You were growing, even when the lessons hurt.

And yes, there were moments that bruised you, moments that broke you,
moments that made you forget your own worth.
But even in the darkest places, something,
a child's voice, a warning, a whisper, a flash of clarity,
called you back to yourself.

You survived what should have silenced you.
You kept going when you didn't know how.
You turned around when you needed saving.
You saw the truth when it finally revealed itself.

These were your caterpillar years,
messy, painful, confusing, holy.
Years that prepared you, even without your permission,
for the wings you were destined to grow.

As you close this chapter, remember:
You were never weak.
You were becoming.
And the story is still unfolding,
beautifully, bravely, and entirely yours.

Chapter Three:
The Caterpillar, Adolescence and Hard Lessons

When the Truth Won't Let You Stay

A caterpillar's purpose is simple: to consume, to grow, to take in everything around it, often without knowing why. It does not yet know its beauty, its wings, or its future. It only knows hunger and survival.

Looking back, that was my caterpillar season.
I was still forming, still learning who I was, still absorbing everything, even the things that drained me, depleted me, or quietly chipped away at parts of me I didn't yet know needed saving.

And like a caterpillar, I became nourishment for everyone but myself:

- I fed someone else's ego.
- I fed someone else's comfort.
- I fed someone else's lies.
- I fed someone else's version of love while starving my own.

There is a saying: *how you get them is how you lose them.*

I didn't just hear those words, I lived them. I swallowed them. They echoed through every corner of my life.

Loving someone divided, distracted, or dishonest places a woman in a silent war she never asked to fight. And the cruellest part is not the lies they tell, it's the lies you start telling yourself.

Because chasing truth can become an addiction.

You start scavenging for clues, waiting for confessions, needing answers the way an addict needs a fix. And like any addict, you start lying to yourself:

"I'm fine."
"It's not that bad."
"I can handle it."
"This isn't who I am."

But addiction doesn't release you until you go within, until you face your own reflection and confront the parts of you that accepted crumbs and called it love.

Because here is the quiet, harsh reality:

People only treat you the way you feel about yourself.
They mirror the value you believe you deserve.
They respond to the worth you either honour... or abandon.

While I chased his truth, I avoided my own.
I wanted honesty from someone who didn't have it to give, and I wasn't being honest with myself either. I ignored the whispers in my spirit, the ache in my chest, the neon signs flashing all around me. I accepted the bare minimum because, deep down, I didn't believe I deserved more.

I thought if I held on tighter... prayed harder... loved deeper...

I could turn chaos into stability, lies into loyalty, brokenness into wholeness.

But the truth I needed most was this:

You cannot demand truth from someone while avoiding your own reflection.
You cannot expect someone to value you when you've forgotten your own worth.

So, I stayed.
I stayed even as my peace left every time, he walked out the door.
I stayed even though women always know.
I stayed even as God whispered louder and louder.

And in staying, I became someone I didn't recognize:

- the investigator
- the detective
- the woman who checked, watched, tracked, and proved instead of simply being

Late, night drive, bys.
Hiding behind buildings.
Scrolling through phones.
Arguing with women who owed me nothing.
Digging for proof as if proof could give me peace.

But proof doesn't bring peace.
Truth does.
And truth begins the moment you choose yourself.

As the pain intensified, darker thoughts crept in, thoughts that did not come from God. Thoughts that warned me staying might cost me everything: my dignity, my mind, my spirit... even my life.

And before I ended up on *First 48*, I had a burst of clarity:
I am claustrophobic, and orange does not look good on me.

That tiny moment of humour in the middle of heartbreak woke something inside me.
It reminded me that even wounded, I still had worth. I still had a life worth saving.

Then God, faithful, patient, and persistent, sent confirmation after confirmation:

Confirmation One: A student mentioned his sister's home in Virginia. I went. It was peaceful, too peaceful for the woman I believed I was.

Confirmation Two: A family friend needed a ride to Virginia. All expenses paid. Another door opened.

Confirmation Three: A dream, vivid and divine, telling me I had to leave Syracuse by July 4th.

Confirmation Four: A little girl in a Jeep waving goodbye. Later, I realized she was me, finally releasing what had been breaking me.

Final Confirmation: *The Girl, the Dad, and the Pearls.*
I had been holding onto plastic love, afraid to release what was counterfeit, never knowing God had something real waiting for me.

And when God sends signs like that, you either surrender or you suffer.

So, I surrendered.

I walked out with one suitcase, my children, and a heart trembling not from fear, but from freedom.

And that moment, when my feet crossed the threshold, my metamorphosis began.

I entered the chrysalis: the sacred space of breaking down, dissolving, and becoming.
Because a caterpillar must completely fall apart before it becomes a butterfly.

The old self cannot survive the transformation.
It must dissolve so something greater can rise.

And so did I.

 Chapter Three: Reflection Journal

The Caterpillar: Adolescence and Hard Lessons

Reflection Questions

1. What "caterpillar habits" did I develop in my younger years, patterns of survival, people, pleasing, or shrinking, that I am now ready to release?

   (Where did I learn to feed everyone but myself?)

   _____

   _____

   _____

   _____

2. When I look back at the moments, I ignored my intuition, what was that inner voice trying to tell me, and how can I honour it now?

   _____

   _____

   _____

   _____

3. What truths about myself, my worth, and my future am I finally ready to step into?

   (Even if they feel new, shaky, or unfamiliar.)

   _____

   _____

   _____

   _____

 # Chapter Three, Affirmation

"I honour the girl who survived, but I am becoming the woman who chooses truth, peace, and self-worth."

 ## Guided Prompt

Take a deep breath and write freely:

Describe the moment in your life when you realized you deserved more than someone's half, love, half, truths, or half, effort. What shifted inside you? What did that awakening feel like?

Let it pour out, your voice, your honesty, your becoming.

 **Closing Encouragement**

You were never meant to stay in the place where you were starving.
You are not the girl who settled, silenced herself, or dimmed her light just to be chosen.

You are the woman who walked away with trembling hands and a courageous heart.
The woman who said, "I choose me", even when it scared her.

Your chrysalis season is not punishment.
It is protection.
It is preparation.
It is rebirth.

Keep going. You are becoming someone you've never met but always hoped to be.

Chapter Four:

The Breaking Before the Becoming

When Life Tries to Destroy You, But God Has Already Decided You Will Rise

efore I ever stepped into my chrysalis, I was already unravelling. Pieces of me were slipping through my own fingers, and I was fighting to hold together a heart that had been breaking in slow motion. Some storms don't roar when they arrive, no thunder, no lightning, no warning, and you don't even have time to grab a Snickers.

And nothing cuts quite like hearing the words:
"I love you... but I'm not in love with you."
Nothing bruises a woman's spirit like being called a "good woman," yet somehow never good enough to be chosen. It wasn't a clean cut, it was a slow, jagged scraping across the soul.

He told me he didn't like the conviction that came with being with me. That my presence made him uncomfortable, not because I harmed him, but because being around me held up a mirror he didn't want to face. He preferred a woman who didn't disrupt his comfort, challenge his shadows, or illuminate the excuses he'd grown comfortable resting in.

And here's the part most men never seem to recognize:

Sometimes a woman leaves long before she walks out the door.
I was gone mentally, physically, and emotionally long before he ever noticed. I had shut down piece by piece, quietly, slowly, painfully. I was going through the motions of a marriage, but the truth is... I was tired. Tired of trying. Tired of carrying the weight alone. Tired of explaining wounds he had no intention of acknowledging. Tired of dying internally while pretending externally.

And the heartbreaking part?

He never even noticed my absence while I was still standing right in front of him.

I had to swallow that bitter pill whole. And listen, whoever said "what doesn't kill you makes you stronger" never choked on a pill that big with no water.

The Collapse Before the Climb

I ran into my grandmother's arms, and the moment she held me, I cried tears she recognized instantly, tears she knew because she had cried them too. The kind passed down through generations of women who loved hard, hurt deeply, and kept going anyway. The kind that cut like a double, edged sword, slicing through every layer of my heart. It felt like walking barefoot on broken glass while carrying the whole weight of my world on my back.

In her embrace, something ancient rose inside me. A whisper that sounded like the voices of every woman who came before me:

"The cycle may reach you, but it will not keep you."
"The pain may be generational, but the healing will be too."

But even with those truths, the days that followed were heavy.
Breathless.
Dark.

It felt like drowning in slow motion.
My weight dropped.
Sleep clocked out on me.
My thoughts spun circles until they bruised my mind.
Every inhale felt like grief was sitting on my chest with crossed legs and an attitude.

Life will distract you sometimes, with heartbreak, with confusion, with pain so loud it tries to drown out your purpose.
Not because you're weak.
Not because the storm is stronger than you.
But because your next season requires a version of you that cannot be built on old wounds.

A Mother's Love: The First Resurrection

One evening, my mother showed up unannounced, sent by God, escorted by intuition. There is nothing on earth like a praying mother, and nothing like a mother who can sense your pain through walls, distance, and silence.

She stepped into my room, saw my face, and her whole spirit shifted.

She didn't ask questions.
She didn't need explanations.
She went straight to war.

She laid hands on me and prayed, not those polite "Lord bless the food" prayers.

No.

She prayed heaven down.

She prayed the ancestors awake.

She prayed like she was telling hell itself to back up off her child.

She declared:

"You will live and not die."

"This heartbreak is not your grave."

"God's work in you is not finished."

Then she said, gently but firmly, "Open your mouth."

But grief had tied knots around my throat so tight I couldn't make a sound.

So, she did something bold, holy, and fierce, something only a mother who refuses to bury her daughter would do:

She breathed into me.

Mouth to mouth.

Spirit to spirit.

A divine CPR.

Something shifted.

Something awakened.

I inhaled, really inhaled, for the first time in weeks.

Not just oxygen...

Hope.

It wasn't dramatic or cinematic.

It was sacred.

In that breath I knew:
I will not die here.
Not in this heartbreak.
Not in this shame.
Not in the place where someone else walked away from me.

The Humour That Saves Us

And listen... somewhere between the tears and the prayers, a thought popped into my mind that I swear came straight from God with a side of humour:

"Girl... you are dramatic, but you are not done."

And for a moment, I almost laughed at myself.
Almost.

Because even in heartbreak, even in our darkest moments, God will slip in a reminder that you are still His child, and His children don't stay buried.

The Breaking Before the Becoming

This was not the end.
This was the breaking,
the necessary breaking,
before the becoming.

I was entering my chrysalis season.
Not to hide,
but to heal.
Not to disappear,
but to transform.

Not to shrink,
but to rise.

Because even in the breaking, wings were forming.
Even in the darkness, new strength was blooming.
Even in the hurt, God was preparing me for the woman I was destined
to become.

A caterpillar doesn't know it's becoming a butterfly while it's dissolving.
It feels like dying.
It feels like the end.
But it is actually becoming.
And so was I.

 # Chapter Four: Reflection Journal

The Breaking Before the Becoming

Reflection Questions

1. What moment in my life felt like "the breaking", the point where everything fell apart, and what did that breaking reveal about who I truly was?
   (What was God stripping away so something new could rise?)

   _____

   _____

   _____

   _____

2. Who or what breathed life back into me when I could no longer breathe for myself?
   (A person, a prayer, a memory, a whisper, a knowing...)

   _____

   _____

   _____

   _____

3. How has pain tried to convince me I was finished, and what evidence in my own life proves that I rose anyway?

   _____

   _____

   _____

   _____

Chapter Four, Affirmation

"My breaking did not destroy me. It rebuilt me. What tried to bury me became the ground where my wings began to grow."

Guided Prompt

Take a moment, breathe deeply, and write from your heart:

Describe a time when someone else's rejection made you question your worth. What did that experience teach you about the woman you are becoming? How did God use that moment to redirect, protect, or awaken something in you?

Let the truth come through, raw, messy, holy, and real.

Chapter Four, Closing Encouragement

There are moments in a woman's life that feel like endings,
when love breaks, when hope cracks, when identity dissolves in your hands.

But hear this truth: **you were never breaking apart... you were breaking open.**

Every tear watered the ground beneath your future.
Every sleepless night carved space for your resurrection.
Every "I'm not in love with you" pushed you closer to the God who has always loved you without condition.

You are not the woman who stayed buried in heartbreak.
You are the woman who inhaled hope again.
You are the woman who rose.
You are the woman who is still becoming.

Your chrysalis is not your coffin.
It is your birthplace.

Keep going. There is beauty forming in you that you cannot yet see, but you will.

Chapter Five:

The Chrysalis: When God Covers What the World Cannot Heal

"When a mother heals, she heals generations."
— **African Proverb**

July 4th was approaching fast, and fear had its hands wrapped tightly around my throat. Not the kind of fear that flutters and disappears, but the kind that sits heavy on your chest, burrows into your bones, and rewires your very breath. The kind that convinces your mind of lies your spirit knows aren't true.

Fear whispered to me like a familiar friend:
Stay. It's safer here. You're not ready. You'll fail. You can't do this.

I wanted to obey. I wanted to follow God's voice. But my thoughts were spiralling, fast, loud, relentless. Every time I imagined walking toward freedom, my mind painted it as disaster. It felt like a war was breaking loose inside my head, chaotic, noisy, nonstop. It reminded me of watching *Tom and Jerry*, where the tiny, good angel shows up on one shoulder and the mischievous bad angel pops up on the other. Except in my mind, they weren't just arguing, they were chasing each other, throwing emotions like frying pans, knocking over my peace, and causing a ruckus I couldn't quiet.

The good angel whispered, *Go. Gods got you.*
The bad one hissed, *Don't move. You'll fall apart. You're not ready.*

And there I stood, caught between faith and fear, feeling like the cartoon version of myself was being tossed around while real, life anxiety tightened its grip. My hands trembled. My stomach knotted. Sleep became a stranger. Counting sheep wasn't working anymore, those sheep were tired, and I was still wide awake. I would watch the sun rise in the morning, not because I welcomed a new day, but because I hadn't slept through the night that came before it. Even when I tried to pray, fear pressed its hand over my mouth. And I sank into silence.

I knew I had to leave, but fear wrapped chains around my feet. It's a cruel kind of suffering, wanting freedom but being terrified to reach for it.

Then the dream returned, a giant finger flipping through the pages of my life like a book, stopping sharply on July 4th. Not gently. Not softly. Sharply. With purpose. A divine warning. A spiritual deadline. A whisper from Heaven: *If you do not leave by this date, the consequences will follow.*

Not punishment, but the natural unravelling that comes when your spirit knows the truth and your feet refuse to move.

Even then, fear gripped tighter. I imagined missing the bus. Losing my children. Failing in Virginia. Starting from nothing. Meeting strangers. Sleeping in unfamiliar places. Fear painted every worst, case scenario in vivid, relentless detail. I wanted to stay in the familiar, even though the familiar was slowly killing me.

Then, a spark, a small, stubborn whisper that wasn't mine, rose inside me: *Do it afraid.*

And something broke open. I realized fear was never the enemy. Fear was the test. The threshold. The doorway between bondage and becoming. Fear wasn't sent to stop me; it was sent to reveal how much I needed God.

The morning of my departure, I still didn't have money for the bus ticket. Panic tried to return with its old lies: *See? You can't do this. You're unprepared. You're alone.*

Then my phone rang.

"Do you have your ticket yet?"

I admitted, "No... not yet."

"Then stop waiting. You're getting out of there."

Minutes later, paid in full. God moved through the hands of someone who loved me. When I couldn't carry myself, Heaven carried me.

My hands still shook. My heart still raced. My stomach twisted with fear, giving me the kind of bubble guts that made every step feel heavier than the last. But something in me was shifting, a trembling courage rising out of the ashes of fear. I ran, literally ran, to the bus terminal. I nearly missed the last bus. My legs felt like sand. I was crying before I even sat down. Fear had tried to kill me, but God refused to let it.

An elderly woman beside me glanced over gently. "Are you okay?" she asked.

I lied. "Yes."

She smiled like she knew my grandmother. "I know that cry. You're going to be alright."

She handed me a tissue, but what she really handed me... was reassurance from Heaven.

And then, the moment that sealed everything, fireworks burst across the sky through the bus window. Bright. Loud. Liberating. It was July 4th. Independence Day. Freedom. Physically, emotionally, spiritually. I was leaving bondage on Independence Day. God had timed my breakthrough with a nation's declaration of freedom. That was no coincidence.

Fear had tried to paralyze me. Fear had tried to distract me. Fear had tried to convince me that staying broken was safer than becoming whole.

But when I stepped forward, trembling, crying, uncertain, God covered me with a strength the world could never give.

And that's when my chrysalis began.

The chrysalis is not comfortable. It's not beautiful. It's not glamorous. It is the sacred, holy place where everything that isn't truly you must die, so everything that is you can live.

Unhealed, we bleed on people who didn't cut us. Our pain spills into our parenting. Our trauma strains our relationships. Our wounds echo through our children's hearts. And that is why the African proverb rings so true:

"When a mother heals, she heals generations."

Because when a mother is broken, the whole house feels it. But when she becomes whole, the whole lineage rises.

Inside the chrysalis, God wasn't just healing me. He was healing the generations that would come after me. He was sealing the wounds my children never deserved to inherit. He was rewriting the story my pain tried to author.

I wasn't just leaving a place. I was leaving a pattern. I was leaving a cycle. I was leaving a version of myself who didn't know she deserved better.

And as the bus pulled away, tears still falling, I whispered:

"This is the beginning... not the end."

 **Chapter Five: Reflection Journal**

The Chrysalis: When God Covers What the World Cannot Heal

Reflection Questions

1. What fear in my life has kept me from moving forward, and what truth is God whispering to help me break free from it?
   (Where has fear tried to chain me, and where is faith trying to lead me?)

   _____

   _____

   _____

2. What "Independence Day moment" have I had, a moment when I knew God was pushing me toward freedom even though I felt terrified?
   (How did Heaven step in when I couldn't move on my own?)

   _____

   _____

   _____

3. What generational patterns, wounds, or cycles am I breaking by choosing healing over familiarity?
   (How will my healing change the future for those who come after me?)

   _____

   _____

   _____

 # Chapter Five, Affirmation

"I may tremble, but I move. Fear does not own me. God covers me, carries me, and prepares the generations through me."

 # Guided Healing Prompt

Write freely and honestly:

Describe a moment when fear felt louder than your faith. What did that fear try to tell you, and what did God show you instead? Write about how stepping forward, even trembling, became an act of courage, protection, and generational healing.

Let the ink tell the truth your spirit has been holding.

Chapter Five, Closing Encouragement

The chrysalis is not pretty.
It is tight, dark, quiet, and holy.

It is the place where everything that once wounded you rises to the surface...
not to break you, but to release you.

Fear tried to convince you that staying where you were was safer than
becoming who God created you to be.
But you moved anyway.
Shaking. Crying. Barely breathing.
Still, you moved.

And Heaven met you at every step,
in the phone call,
in the ticket,
in the stranger's kindness,
in the fireworks lighting up your escape,
in the timing only God could orchestrate.

You didn't just leave a house.
You left a history.
You left a version of yourself that fear had been feeding for years.
And by choosing healing, you lit a path for generations who will never
know the battles you fought for them.

Your chrysalis is not punishment,
it is preparation.

You are not breaking down,
you are breaking open.

You are not lost,
you are being remade.

And when the time comes,
when the healing takes root,
when the wings are ready...
you will emerge brighter than the fear that tried to bury you.

You are becoming.
You are rising.
And God is not finished with you, not even close.

Chapter Six:
Inside the Chrysalis – The Unmaking and the Becoming

People love to talk about transformation as if it's a soft, glittering moment, like one day you wake up with wings, and the sun is shining just right. But anyone who knows real healing knows the truth: transformation is not pretty. It is not gentle. And it is not painless.

Inside a real chrysalis, the caterpillar doesn't sleep. It dissolves. Its body liquefies, every part of what it was breaking down so something completely new can form. Nothing remains untouched. Nothing stays the same.

That's what happened to me. When fear finally broke me, when life cornered me and God called me forward, I wasn't stepping into a new season, I was stepping into a chrysalis. A dark, quiet chamber where I couldn't go backward anymore, but I had no idea how to go forward either. That space suspended me, stripped me, and forced me into stillness.

And for the first time in years... I had to stop running.
Running from truth.
Running from pain.
Running from responsibility.
Running from myself.

I had to take my Nikes off and stop sprinting from the very things God needed me to face. Stop treating healing like a race I could outrun.

God didn't just ask me to heal in that season; He asked me to sit with myself. To learn who I was beneath the damage, beneath the survival mode, beneath the masks I didn't even know I was wearing. I had to sit with my silence. I had to sit with my fears. I had to sit with the decisions I made when I didn't know better, and the ones I made when I did.

And most of all, I had to learn the hardest lesson of all: I wasn't alone, even though loneliness lived in my chest like an echo. I wasn't abandoned, even when I felt upheld. And I wasn't broken beyond repair, even when I no longer recognized myself.

Or, as the seasoned generation would say, you can't just *tiptoe through the tulips*. The chrysalis doesn't allow that kind of soft stepping. It doesn't let you hide, dodge, or disappear behind excuses. In fact, it's almost like being placed in a spiritual witness protection program, God tucks you away, removes you from everything familiar, strips away the identities you tried to wear, and hides you in a place where you can't be found by the person you used to be. You're concealed but not forgotten. Hidden, but not lost. Covered, but not running. In that sacred hiding place, the chrysalis forces you to confront the truth until God's voice becomes louder than your shame.

And it wasn't just others I hurt. I had to face how my decisions impacted my parents, the two people who wanted so desperately to save me even when I couldn't save myself. My mother's tears weren't tears disappointment. They were heartbreak. She saw dangers I couldn't see, storms I thought I was strong enough to outrun. But she also knew something I didn't: Some fires can only be survived by walking through them.

And as I navigated this sacred breaking, I saw my father, the man who had always been my protector, my defender, standing on the sidelines, helpless. Helpless in the face of battles he could not fight for me, powerless against the pain that life had placed on my path. The heartbreak wasn't his failure; it was the brutal truth that even the strongest shields can't guard against every storm. His hands were tied, his heart heavy, and yet he loved fiercely in the only way he could. Witnessing his helplessness reminded me that even love sometimes cannot shield us, and that strength isn't always measured by action, but by presence and prayer.

Even in the darkest moments, my parents never stopped believing in the power of prayer over their children. Long after I thought hope was gone, long after I had buried myself under shame and despair, they continued to lift me up in prayer, faithful, relentless, unshaken. Their prayers became invisible threads of protection, guidance, and love that wove through the shadows I was walking through, reminding me that I was never truly alone.

Inside that chrysalis, everything I tried to outrun rose up and demanded to be seen. I had to face the truth about the role I played in hurting another woman and her family, not because I was the source, but because my presence still left a ripple. That truth humbled me in ways I cannot describe.

Then there was the grief, the deep, aching grief, over terminating a pregnancy at a time when I was overwhelmed and emotionally undone. I carried that memory in silence for years, letting the enemy turn it into a weapon against my soul:

"Unworthy."
"Unforgivable."
"Stupid."

Words I believed. Words that chained me.

Inside the chrysalis, I also faced the hardest truth of all, the truth about the mother I used to be. The one who loved deeply but struggled to stay emotionally present. The one who kept her guard high, not out of lack of love, but out of fear of being hurt again. I didn't realize my wounds were bleeding onto my children, touching them in ways I never intended.

There is an African proverb that says:
"The child who is not embraced by the village will burn it down to feel its warmth."

But there is another one, one that became the heartbeat of my chrysalis: "A healed mother raises nations; an unhealed mother bleeds on everyone she loves."

Inside the chrysalis, I realized how much I had bled, not intentionally, not maliciously, but out of pain I never tended to. Out of wounds I tried to pretend didn't exist. Out of battles I never paused long enough to process.

Yet even in all that truth, telling, even in the unmaking of who I once was, God did not condemn me. He comforted me. He showed me I could:

Grieve the woman I used to be.
Forgive the mother who didn't know better.
Heal the daughter who caused accidental harm.
And apologize, to myself, to my children, to my past.

None of this happened overnight. Healing isn't magic; it's surrender. Slowly, silently, faithfully, everything heavy in me began to dissolve, not disappear, transform.

This was the dying. But it was also the beginning of the becoming. Inside the darkness, I wasn't being destroyed. I was being rebuilt.

 **Chapter Six: Reflection Journal**

Inside the Chrysalis – The Unmaking and the Becoming

Reflection Questions

1. What parts of myself am I still running from, and what would happen if I stopped running and faced them with God's guidance? *(Where in my life am I avoiding the truth that could set me free?)*

2. How have the prayers, presence, or love of others, like parents, mentors, or friends, protected and strengthened me even when I didn't feel supported? *(Who or what has been the unseen thread holding me together?)*

3. In what ways can I embrace my unmaking as the doorway to my becoming? *(How can I allow God to dissolve what no longer serves me so the new me can rise?)*

 # Chapter Six, Affirmation

"I am not broken beyond repair. Every layer that falls away is a step toward the woman I am meant to become. I trust God to rebuild me in His time and His way."

 # Guided Prompt

Take a quiet moment and write without censoring yourself:

Reflect on a decision, regret, or wound that has lingered in your life. How has it shaped you? What can you surrender to God today so that you may emerge renewed, whole, and free? How can you see your chrysalis as sacred rather than painful?

Chapter Six, Closing Encouragement

Transformation is not gentle.

It is not instant.

It is not always beautiful in the moment.

The chrysalis is dark, quiet, and uncomfortable, but it is sacred.

It strips away the masks, the running, the excuses, and the old identities.

In this space, God is not breaking you to punish you.

He is unmaking the parts of you that no longer serve your purpose.

He is rebuilding, piece by piece, layer by layer.

Your grief, your mistakes, your unhealed moments, none of it is wasted.

It is the soil from which your wings will grow.

It is the furnace forging your courage.

It is the sacred chamber where your becoming begins.

You are not being destroyed.

You are being remade.

You are not alone.

You are being prepared to rise.

Keep breathing, keep surrendering, keep trusting. Your wings are forming.

Chapter Seven:

Stepping Out of the Tombs: The Moment I Chose Freedom

Condemnation had lived with me for so long it felt like a room-mate, one that never paid rent but always took up space. It whispered in the dark corners of my mind, shaped the way I moved through life, and convinced me that shame was my permanent address.

One day, something inside me stirred, a quiet urgency almost like a nudge from God, urging me to look up the word *condemned*. When I saw it defined as "sentenced to a particular punishment, especially death," something inside me cracked open. Because that was exactly how I had been living, spiritually, emotionally, mentally, as if someone had already written the sentence for my life. A life I nearly surrendered to pain, to guilt, to cycles I didn't know how to exit. A life weighed down by mistakes made by a younger girl, hungry, unprotected, confused, and unaware of her own worth.

I realized that living under condemnation is like living in a building deemed unfit for use: we tear ourselves down when life goes wrong. And yet, one day the Spirit whispered to me: *Why are you living in condemnation?*

Who are you to tear yourself down? As long as there is breath in your body, there is hope.

I could breathe again, and with every breath, claim the life that had been waiting for me all along. Like in my Toni Braxton voice, *I could breathe again, breathe again.*

Growing up in the church, I had heard the story of the woman caught in adultery. Women with complicated stories, women like me, women who made imperfect choices, loved the wrong way, or stayed the wrong time, were stoned. Silenced. Buried under shame. And suddenly I saw myself in her: judged by many, understood by few, yet worthy of grace long before I even knew how to receive it.

As I sat in that revelation, Kirk Franklin's *"Imagine Me"* began to play, and the lyrics settled over me like a balm for my soul:

"Letting go of the past... Glad, I have another chance... My heart will dance... Cause I don't have to read that page again. Imagine me, being free. Trusting you, totally. Finally, I can imagine me. I admit, it was hard to see... You being in love with someone like me. Finally, I can imagine me."
—Kirk Franklin

The song didn't just play around me; it played through me. Every note whispered a truth I had been too afraid to claim I could release the shame, the guilt, the self, condemnation that had held me hostage. I was no longer condemned. I no longer had to carry the weight of past mistakes. I no longer had to read that page again. My heart could dance. My spirit could soar. My life could be claimed fully, freely, and without fear.

That day, I decided:
I would put the stones down.

I would stop stoning myself.

I would leave the graveyard.

I would choose life.

I would imagine myself fully, completely, undeniably free.

And for the first time, I breathed like a woman reborn. Not the condemned woman. Not the abandoned wife. Not the mother who failed. Not the broken girl. But a woman whose spiritual account had been restored. A woman forgiven. A woman alive. A woman free.

This was the moment the chrysalis cracked. This was the moment I began to emerge.

 Chapter Seven: Reflection Journal

Stepping Out of the Tombs – The Moment I Chose Freedom

Reflection Questions

1. In what ways have you been living under condemnation, allowing shame, guilt, or past mistakes to define you?
   (Where are you holding stones that you need to put down?)

   _____

   _____

   _____

2. What truths are you ready to claim about your worth, your freedom, and your capacity to forgive yourself?
   (How can you begin imagining yourself fully, without fear or self-judgment?)

   _____

   _____

   _____

3. What does freedom look like for you, and what steps can you take to step out of the tombs of your past into life, hope, and restoration?

   _____

   _____

   _____

 # Chapter Seven, Affirmation

"I release the weight of past mistakes. I am forgiven, restored, and free. My life is mine to live fully, and I step boldly into the light God has prepared for me."

 # Guided Prompt

Write freely for 10–15 minutes:

Reflect on a moment when shame or self, condemnation has held you captive. What would it feel like to lay down those stones and step fully into freedom? How can you embrace the woman, man, or child you are becoming today without looking back?

 Chapter Seven, Closing Encouragement

Freedom is not a destination; it is a choice.

It is choosing to stop carrying the weight of mistakes, regrets, or self, judgment.
It is releasing the stones you have held against yourself for too long.
It is stepping out of the tombs of fear, condemnation, and silence into life, hope, and joy.

You do not have to read that page again.
You do not have to stay where you have been.
Your spirit can dance. Your heart can soar.
Your life can be fully claimed, freely, boldly, beautifully.

Take a deep breath. Let go. Step forward. Your freedom is waiting.

Chapter Won:
Rebirth: Seeing My Wings for the First Time

*E*ight is the number of new beginnings, and that is why this chapter is not Chapter Eight. It is Chapter **Won**. Because this is where everything shifted. This is where I chose me. This is where I truly won.

Fighting My Way Out and Fighting My Way Through, these words became the quiet rhythm of my rebirth. I didn't wake up one morning perfectly whole. Healing didn't arrive dramatically, all at once. It came in soft whispers, in tiny victories, in quiet awakenings that reminded me:

You're still here.
You're still rising.
You're still winning.

The Night I Remembered Joy

One night at work, Rob, one of the boys at the group home, was on a roll. His jokes were outrageous, his impersonations ridiculous, and before I knew it, I was laughing so hard I could barely breathe.

And right there, in the middle of that moment, something inside me cracked open.

I realized I couldn't remember the last time I had laughed like that, full, free, unfiltered.

In that laughter, I heard a gentle, yet undeniable message rise inside me:

I will laugh again.
I will live again.
I will win again.

That night, something in me awakened. A small healing. A spark. A flicker of wings beginning to stretch.

When My Heart Began to Wake Up

After years of distractions, wrong choices, and broken patterns, God began placing people in my life to remind me that I wasn't invisible. That I was worthy. That I was lovable.

And then, quietly, there was him, steady, attentive, grounded. He didn't rush or overwhelm me. He simply showed up with presence, safety, and a softness I had forgotten existed.

But this time, I didn't lose myself. This time, I didn't run headfirst into old traps. This time, I remembered:

I've won too much to lose myself again.

Even the dreams I had kept tucked away, the quiet vision of a man kneeling, offering partnership, offering love, were all part of what God had been aligning behind the scenes long before I ever recognized it. And then one day, as I was moving through an ordinary moment at work, the Spirit whispered to me so clearly:

"Your husband is about to walk through the door."

And within seconds of that voice settling in my spirit, the door chimed *beep, beep*. I didn't think much of it, until I looked up and saw him. The shock of seeing him standing there hit me so hard that everything on my desk went tumbling to the floor. My heart jumped. My breath caught. He rushed toward me, asking gently, *"Are you okay?"* as he knelt to help gather the scattered papers.

It was as if I had seen a ghost, familiar yet unexpected, like a promise walking on two feet.

And in that instant, beneath the surprise and the pounding in my chest, my spirit recognized something before my mind ever could:

A new beginning had just walked through the door.

The Beginning of Us

The first moments with him were quiet miracles. A ride through the city. Christmas lights. Small conversations. Deep breaths I didn't even know I had been holding.

For the first time in a long time, I felt myself unfolding, not rushing, not performing, not shrinking. Just being. That was my victory too.

Becoming Mrs. Martin, and Winning Myself Back

Now, approaching fifty, I see everything with clarity: I am finally seeing my wings. And I won every feather.

All the years of fighting, breaking, rebuilding, relearning, untangling, crying, praying, they led me here. To wholeness. To softness. To strength.

I am becoming:

- A better wife
- A better mother
- A better daughter
- A better sister, aunt, niece, cousin, friend
- A better me

Where Motherhood Meets My Victory

For so long, I mothered from empty places, giving from scarcity, loving from survival, hoping from fear. I carried guilt that never belonged to me and the weight of perfection no human could ever achieve.

But healing taught me something motherhood had been whispering all along:

When I win myself back, my children win too.

They don't need a perfect mother. They need a present one. A joyful one. A whole one. Now I laugh with them differently. I listen more deeply. I hold space without losing myself. I mother from a place of fullness, not fragments. That is one of the greatest "I won's" of my life.

Forgiveness as Wings

Forgiveness became the invisible wings that lifted me. Not because those who hurt me deserved it, but because I deserved freedom. Not because I condoned the pain inflicted, but because I refused to carry it anymore.

Forgiveness is a conscious, deliberate decision to release the heavy chains of resentment, bitterness, or the desire for vengeance. It is a choice to no longer let the actions of others, and even my own past mistakes, anchor me in a cage of shame.

I learned to extend grace, first to myself. To release the girl who made choices out of fear, out of hunger, out of survival. To forgive the woman I was when I didn't know better. To forgive the people who hurt me, not to excuse them, but to unburden my soul.

Grace became the wind beneath my wings. It taught me that the same Spirit who whispered life over my broken heart can whisper love and freedom over every corner of my past.

Standing in My Womanhood

Through him, I learned that softness is not weakness. That femininity is power. That I am divine, chosen, seen. My worth is no longer borrowed. It belongs to me. Forged in fire, shaped by grace.

I won my voice.
I won my healing.
I won my motherhood.
I won my life back.
I see my wings now. And I am no longer afraid to fly.

Eight is the number of new beginnings. And this is **Chapter Won**, because I won me back.

 # Chapter Won: Reflection Journal

Rebirth — Seeing My Wings for the First Time

Reflection Questions

1. Where in your life are you ready to experience rebirth, growth, or a new beginning?

   (What areas of your heart, mind, or spirit are ready to awaken?)

   _____

   _____

   _____

   _____

2. What small victories or moments of joy have reminded you that you are still rising and still winning?

   (How can you celebrate the wins you may have overlooked?)

   _____

   _____

   _____

   _____

3. In what ways can you practice forgiveness and grace, for yourself and others, to lift your wings fully?

   (What chains of resentment or self, blame are you ready to release?)

   _____

   _____

   _____

   _____

 ## Chapter Won, Affirmation

"I am becoming whole. I am free. I am worthy of joy, love, and abundance. My wings are stretching, and I am ready to soar."

 ## Guided Prompt

Write freely for 10–15 minutes:

Reflect on a moment when you felt your wings beginning to stretch, whether through healing, joy, laughter, or grace. How can you nurture that growth? What does winning yourself back look like for you today?

_____

_____

_____

_____

_____

_____

_____

_____

_____

_____

_____

_____

_____

 Chapter Won, Closing Encouragement

Rebirth is quiet, patient, and intentional. It doesn't always come with big moments, sometimes it starts with a small laugh, a little hope, or one choice to take yourself back. Your wings have been forming through every tear, every prayer, every lesson, and every brave step you've taken. Celebrate every victory, big or small. Forgive yourself, forgive others, and let your softness be your strength.

You are winning.

You are rising.

You are free.

And your wings are ready

Chapter Nine:

Living Selflessly: It Begins and Ends with Me

For so long, I believed my purpose was to be everything to everyone else. I was the daughter who carried the silent weight of my parents' worries, the friend who stayed late absorbing pain that wasn't mine. I was the mother who poured herself out so completely for her children that I forgot to breathe, and the wife who bent, forgave, and reshaped herself endlessly to fix what only I could not control.

I was running on empty, pouring from a cracked cup, and wondering why life still felt heavy. But life, in its quiet wisdom, will always circle back to teach you what you missed the first time: true strength is not in endless giving, it is in being whole. And the truth I finally embraced is both radical and simple: everything begins and ends selflessly with me.

Selflessness is not sacrificing yourself to the point of disappearance. It is not bleeding just to keep others warm. True selflessness is rooted in fullness, nurturing your own heart, mind, and soul so deeply that what you give flows from abundance, not exhaustion.

I am learning to honour my boundaries, my time, my emotions, and my spirit. Saying no is no longer guilt; it is wisdom. Taking a pause is no longer weakness; it is sacred. Choosing myself first does not abandon the people I love, it teaches them a new standard of what is possible. It shows my children, my husband, and my community that life is richest when you recognize your own worth.

And then, years later, unexpectedly, I received an apology. One I never thought would come. One I didn't realize I still needed. And even though I had already begun walking the long, tender road of healing, that apology softly closed a door I had been holding open with questions, doubts, and quiet hurt I hadn't resolved in my mind.

Closure can be a blessing. But closure is also a choice.

Because when the apology finally arrives, whether whispered through tears or delivered clumsily, imperfectly, you face a new question:
Do I hold on to it... or do I let it go?

Here is what I learned:
The apology is not the healing.
What you do with it is.

You can accept it without reopening old wounds.
You can release it without bitterness.
You can honour it without inviting old pain back into your home.
You can move forward with gratitude, not attachment.

An apology doesn't rewrite the past, but it can release the weight of it. And sometimes, that release is all your spirit needs to rise.

And as I stood there holding words, I never thought I'd hear, I realized another truth I had grown into I could have forgiven and rehearsed and regurgitated every past hurt and every sin inflicted on me, but forgiveness was never for them, it was **for me**. I refused to keep people hostage to their mistakes, just as I refused to bind myself to mine. I offered grace, even where closure was absent. And I apologized, too, because no, I wasn't perfect. But grace allowed me to respect my own growth, acknowledge my missteps, and move forward without shame.

That is the quiet power of selflessness rooted in wholeness:
It frees you to love, release, heal, and rise without losing yourself.

I am discovering that my dreams, my joy, my peace, they are not indulgences. They are the fertile soil from which love, generosity, and purpose bloom. When I give from a place of overflow, what I offer is no longer hollow or hurried, it is transformative, enduring, alive.

For the first time in my life, I am not afraid to be whole.
I am not afraid to let my heart, my voice, and my wings be seen.
I am learning to live selflessly, not from depletion, but from overflow.
From a deep, abiding source of love within me that can never again be drained.

Because it truly does begin and end with me.
And in that truth, I have found freedom.
I have found power.
I have found a life no longer borrowed, no longer shaped by fear or expectation,
but a life that is genuinely mine.

A life worth soaring into...
wings wide,
heart open,
spirit unbound.

 # Chapter Nine: Reflection Journal

Living Selflessly — It Begins and Ends with Me

Reflection Questions

1. **Where in your life have you been pouring from an empty cup?**
   (What areas or relationships are asking you to refill yourself first?)

   _____

   _____

   _____

   _____

2. **How can practicing selflessness from a place of wholeness transform your relationships and your life?**
   (What boundaries or daily practices can support this shift?)

   _____

   _____

   _____

   _____

3. **What does choose yourself first look like in your everyday life, without guilt or fear?**
   (How can self, care become a radical act of love for yourself and others?)

   _____

   _____

   _____

   _____

 ## Chapter Nine, Affirmation

"I am whole. I am abundant. I give from fullness, not depletion. My selfless-ness begins with me, and in honouring myself, I honour everyone I love."

 ## Guided Prompt

Write freely for 10–15 minutes:

Reflect on a moment when you chose yourself first, even slightly, and how it impacted you and those around you. How can you continue to practice living selflessly from abundance instead of depletion?

Chapter Nine, Closing Encouragement

Selflessness is not about giving until you disappear, it is about rising fully and honouring your heart, your boundaries, and your spirit. When you live from a place of wholeness, your love expands, your impact deepens, and your presence becomes a true gift rather than a burden. Remember that everything begins and ends with you. Fill your cup, protect your peace, and honour your joy. Because when you rise, you lift generations; when you soar, you inspire others to fly. Your wings are wide, your heart is open, and your spirit remains beautifully unbound.

Chapter Ten:

Not the Last Chapter: Carrying the Truth Forward

(Because every ending leads back to Chapter Won Again)

Socrates once said, *"I am the wisest man alive, for I know one thing, and that is that I know nothing."*

And the older I grow, the more I understand the sacred humility in those words. Healing, growth, and rebirth do not come with perfection or certainty. They come with the willingness to learn and unlearn, to rise and fall, and to rise again. Wisdom is not found in having all the answers, but in staying open, teachable, willing to begin again each time life calls you back to yourself.

As I close this chapter of my story, I want you to hold one truth close: my journey is not a fairy tale. It is not a perfect timeline of victories or a smooth path to recovery. It is raw, messy, painful, beautiful, and sacred, and it is far from over. Because with every ending, God places the pen gently back into our hands. No matter what came before, you always have the power to return to Chapter Won Again, the moment you reclaim yourself, your joy, and your life.

Life will continue to test you. Storms will return. Old whispers of shame, doubt, rejection, and fear may try to rise again. But here is what I need you to carry forward:

You are not defined by your past.

The heartbreaks, betrayals, mistakes, and moments of shame, those were chapters, not your ending. They do not determine your worth. They do not hold the final word. Because the moment you rise again, you step back into Chapter Won, the place where you win.

Healing is a choice. It is rarely neat, rarely easy. And like a butterfly emerging from its chrysalis, the process can feel dangerous and uncertain. When a butterfly breaks free, its wings are soft, wet, fragile, and weak. It must flap and push for hours to strengthen them. If it does not fight through that vulnerable stage, its wings will never open, and it will never fly.

Transformation is exactly like that, messy, demanding, terrifying at times. Full of moments where everything inside you whispers, *"I can't."* But every push, every flap, every trembling inch forward prepares you for flight. Every small step returns you to Chapter Won, where you choose yourself again and again.

Freedom begins, and ends, with you.

You cannot pour love into others from an empty heart. So, care for your spirit. Protect your joy. Honor your story. And honouring your story means honouring it in truth, not in the lies we tell ourselves when we play the victim, minimize our part, or hide behind excuses, but in the truth that frees, restores, and rebuilds.

Because the deepest form of self, betrayal is denying your own truth. Dostoevsky said it with piercing clarity:

"Above all, don't lie to yourself. The man who lies to himself and listens to his own lie comes to a point that he cannot distinguish the truth within him, or around him, and so loses all respect for himself and for others. And having no respect he ceases to love."

When you stop lying to yourself, when you stop rehearsing the excuses, the justifications, and the versions of the story that keep you stuck, you reclaim your power. You reclaim your clarity. You reclaim the ability to love yourself and others honestly, fully, and without distortion.

That is where freedom begins.
That is where healing takes root.
That is where real, abundant, unshakable love is born.

Some truths are sacred. Not every detail needs an audience. Your deepest wounds do not need to become public lessons. Some healing is meant to sit quietly in your soul, strengthening you in private. Softness is not weakness. Strength can be gentle. Vulnerability can be brave. And you, yes, you, are capable of rising from any storm, any chrysalis, any broken place, into a life bigger, fuller, and more beautiful than you ever imagined.

Back at One

Sometimes, even when we believe our work is finished, when we think we have climbed the mountain, healed the wound, or claimed the victory, life whispers a gentle truth: **start back at one.**

In African culture, we honour the symbol of **Sankofa**, a bird whose head looks backward while its body moves forward. Sankofa teaches that to grow, we must return to what we left behind, reclaim the wisdom, heal the wounds, and carry forward only what serves us. Looking back is not weakness; it is sacred. It is how we recover what was lost, restore what was broken, and remember who we were before life tried to make us forget.

This is the heartbeat of Chapter Won.
Just as Brian McKnight sings in *Back at One*:
"If ever I believe my work is done, then I'll start back at one."

Life gives us the same invitation, not because we failed, but because we have more rising, more becoming, more unfolding ahead. Chapter Won is the place you return to when you've grown deeply but know there is still more inside you waiting to bloom. A place to breathe, renew, and choose yourself again.

Your story, your growth, your wings, none of these are the conclusion. They are the invitation:

- to keep going
- to keep healing
- to keep emerging
- to keep flying

And as Sankofa reminds us, what you learn on your journey is not just for you. When you see someone struggling where you once stood, remember this: **your story may be their lifeline.**
And when you share from a healed place, rather than from hurt, you become strength, hope, and light for someone else's Chapter Won.

So when life feels overwhelming, when you feel lost or unsure, hold this truth close:

You are always one choice away from Chapter Won Again.

And every time you choose yourself,
every time you rise,
every time you begin again,
you win.

 # Chapter Ten: Reflection Journal

Not the Last Chapter – Carrying the Truth Forward

Top 3 Reflection Questions

1. **When has fear, doubt, or rejection tried to hold you still?**
   (How did you push through, even when it felt impossible, like a butterfly drying its wings?)

   _____

   _____

   _____

2. **How can you remind yourself to return to Chapter Won Again, even after setbacks or endings?**
   (What practices, affirmations, or actions help you claim yourself and your life repeatedly?)

   _____

   _____

   _____

3. **What does "freedom begins and ends with you" mean in your current life?**
   (Where can you protect your joy, honor your story, and care for your spirit more intentionally?)

   _____

   _____

   _____

 # Chapter Ten: Affirmation

"I am capable of rising again and again. Each choice I make to honour myself is a return to Chapter Won. I am free, whole, and ready to soar, no matter how many chapters have come before."

 ## Guided Prompt

Write for 10–15 minutes:

Reflect on a time when life challenged you to start over or rise again. How did you find the courage to keep moving forward? How can you carry that strength into your present and future chapters?

Chapter Ten, Closing Encouragement

Endings are never truly final. Every ending is an invitation to return to Chapter Won Again. Life will test you, your wings will tremble, and storms may rise, but every push, every flap, every step forward is preparing you to fly.

You are the author of your story. You hold the pen. You can always start back at one.

Carry your truth forward. Protect your joy. Honor your story. Rise. Fly. Begin again. Because you've already won.

Final Reflection & Action:
Stepping Fully into Your Wings, Chapter *Won*

*Y*ou have weathered storms, faced shadows, and sat in the stillness of your own soul. You have lived through chapters that tried to break you, silence you, and convince you that your story was finished. But every time life tried to write your ending, you picked up the pen again.

This is the heart of **Chapter Won**, the realization that the chapters meant to defeat you became the chapters you *won*.

Every heartbreak, betrayal, rejection, and moment of shame wasn't a tombstone. It was a turning point.
Every mistake wasn't a verdict. It was a lesson.
Every fall wasn't a failure. It was a rehearsal for rising.

You didn't just survive those seasons, you *won* them.
And your motherhood is living proof of that victory. Every sacrifice, every late night, every tear you wiped when no one was watching, every moment you loved others while fighting your own battles, that is winning. That is womanhood. That is strength earned, not borrowed.

You have moved from the caterpillar years to the chrysalis, from hiding to healing, from silence to selfhood. And now you stand here, wings wide, heart wiser, spirit unbreakable, because **your last chapter wasn't your final chapter. It was your winning chapter.**

Now is your moment to pause, claim your victory, and step fully into the life you are writing next.

 ## Reflection Questions: Chapter Won Edition

Seeing the Patterns

Which old stories once made you feel unworthy or small, and how will you reclaim them now as proof that you *won*?

Owning Your Growth

What have the hardest seasons taught you about your strength, your motherhood, your faith, and your capacity to love?

Rewriting Your Narrative

How can you reinterpret your heartbreaks, rejections, and trials as evidence of your victory rather than reminders of your pain?

Honouring Your True Self

What does stepping into your authentic, healed self, look like as a woman and as a mother?

Acknowledging Your Wings

In what ways are you already emerging, rising, and winning, and how will you nurture that growth daily?

Action Steps: Living in Your Chapter Won

Daily Affirmation

Speak victory over yourself each morning:
My past was a chapter, but I won it. My story is still unfolding.

Set Boundaries

Protect your peace. Saying "no" is not rejection, it is self, respect.

Intentional Healing

Choose one emotion, memory, or relationship to release or reconcile with this week.
Healing is winning.

Celebrate Small Victories

Every moment of courage, laughter, or self, care is proof that you're already rising.

Create a Freedom Ritual

Journal, pray, meditate, or move, choose what honours your journey and strengthens your wings.

 Closing Reflection: You Already Won

Take a breath.
Hand over your heart.
Feel that steady beat, proof that you made it.

You've walked through seasons that tried to break you, carried weight no one saw, and kept loving even when your heart was tired. That wasn't weakness.
That was courage. That was faith.
That was victory.

You didn't always feel strong or brave. Some days you barely felt like yourself. But you kept showing up, for your children, for your healing, for the woman you were becoming.
That is winning.

Your wings didn't grow in the sunshine.
They grew in the dark,
in quiet tears,
in holding your family together with a fragile heart,
in choosing compassion over anger,
in getting up on days you felt like giving up.

Those moments shaped you.
Those moments crowned you.

Now, as you step into what's next, remember:
You're not here because life was easy.
You're here because you refused to give up.

You are softer, wiser, stronger.
You love deeper.
You walk with fire, forged grace.

And your story?
It's still unfolding.

What felt like the end was your beginning.
What looked like defeat was preparation.
What you thought was your last chapter...
was your Chapter Won.

So carry this gently:
You are allowed to rest.
You are allowed to dream again.
You are allowed to feel joy without fear.
You are allowed to outgrow old versions of yourself.
You are allowed to fly.

You're not behind.
You're not broken.
You're right on time,
arriving as the woman you fought to become.

Walk forward with tenderness.
Walk forward with courage.
Walk forward knowing the truth:

You already won.
And the best of your story is still ahead.

Daily Practice (5–10 minutes): Chapter Won Living

1. **Morning Affirmation**

   Say or write three winning truths:

   I am enough.

   I am free from what tried to break me.

   I honour my heart, my motherhood, and my journey.

2. **Gratitude Moment**

   One thing you're proud of in yourself.
   One thing you appreciate in your life.

3. **Reflection Check, In**

   Ask:

   - Where am I showing up bravely today?
   - Where do I need kindness or patience with myself?

4. **Intentional Action**

   Choose one nourishing act:

   - A boundary
   - Five minutes of journaling
   - A quiet walk
   - Reaching out to someone who lifts you up

Weekly Practice (15–20 minutes)

1. **Review & Release**

   Where did old patterns show up?
   What can you release to lighten your wings?

2. **Celebrate Growth**

   Name three ways you practiced courage, love, or truth this week.

3. **Visioning Your Next Chapter**

   What do you want to welcome in?
   What will you protect?
   Visualize your next chapter, your next *win*.

4. **Sacred Closure**

   Light a candle.
   Play uplifting music.
   Pray, breathe, affirm.
   Honor your wings.

Remember this always:
Growth is not perfect. Some days you will soar. Some days you will crawl. But every day you choose yourself is a victory.
Every day you rise, no matter how slowly, is **Chapter Won**.

And every day your wings grow stronger.

Closing Reflection:
You Already Won

*T*ake a breath. Place your hand over your heart. Feel it, steady, courageous. That rhythm is proof of all you've survived.

You walked through seasons that could have broken you, carried battles no one saw, and continued to love even when your heart was tired. That is not weakness, it is strength. That is victory.

You didn't always feel brave. You didn't always recognize yourself. Yet you showed up, for your children, your healing, your future, the woman you were becoming. That is what winning looks like.

Your wings didn't grow in the sunshine. They grew in the dark, in quiet tears, in moments of fragility, in choosing love and grace over anger and fear. Those moments formed you. Those moments crowned you.

You are not who you were. You are wiser, softer, stronger. Your love is deeper. Your vision clearer. Your spirit moves with grace shaped by fire.

Your story is still unfolding. What once felt like an ending was your beginning. What you thought was your last chapter... was your **Chapter Won**.

Carry this truth:
I am allowed to rest.

I am allowed to dream.

I am allowed to fly.

You are not behind. You are not broken. You are exactly on time.

You already won. And the best of your story is still ahead.

 **Journal**

Brandy Martin

Brandy Martin

Brandy Martin

www.ingramcontent.com/pod-product-compliance
Lightning Source LLC
Chambersburg PA
CBHW070633130626
46555CB00006B/2540